* WE ARE AMERICA *

Japanese Americans

TIFFANY PETERSON

Heinemann Library
Chicago, Illinois

Customer Service 888-454-2279

Visit our website at www.heinemannlibrary.com

Designed by Roslyn Broder
Photo research by Scott Braut
Printed in China by WKT Company Limited

08 07 06 05 04
10 9 8 7 6 5 4 3 2 1

Library of Congress Cataloging-in-Publication Data
Peterson, Tiffany.
  Japanese Americans / Tiffany Peterson.
     p. cm. -- (We are America)
  Summary: An overview of the history and daily lives of Japanese people who immigrated to the United States.
  Includes bibliographical references (p.) and index.
  ISBN 1-4034-5022-6 (lib. bgd.) ISBN 1-4034-5032-3 (pbk.)
  1. Japanese Americans--Juvenile literature. 2. Immigrants--United States--Juvenile literature. 3. United States--Emigration and immigration--Juvenile literature. 4. Japan--Emigration and immigration--Juvenile literature. 5. Japanese Americans--Biography--Juvenile literature. 6. Immigrants--United States--Biography--Juvenile literature. [1. Japanese Americans.] I. Title. II. Series.
  E184.J3P45 2004
  973'.04956--dc22
                              2003021702

Acknowledgments
The author and publisher are grateful to the following for permission to reproduce copyright material:
pp. 4, 5, 28, 29 Courtesy of Joe Yakura; p. 6 C21 Rice Preparation c. 1865 - 1910 by Kusakabe Kimbei/Gift of Mr. and Mrs. John Putnam, Seattle Art Museum, Accession 86.51; pp. 8, 9, 10 Bettmann/Corbis; p. 12 Security Pacific Collection/Los Angeles Public Library; p. 13 PEMCO Webster & Stevens Collection/Museum of History & Industry; pp. 14, 15 Gift of Kenji Yamamoto Family/Japanese American National Museum; p. 16 Corbis; p. 17 National Archives and Records Administration; p. 18 Tony Freeman/Photo Edit; p. 19 Esbin-Anderson/The Image Works; p. 20 Michael S. Yamashita/Corbis; p. 21 Walter Hodges/Stone/Getty Images; p. 22 Joe Carini/The Image Works; p. 23 Shades of Los Angeles/Los Angeles Public Library; pp. 24, 26 Michael Newman/Photo Edit; p. 25 Bill Parsons Photography/MIRA; p. 27 Wolfgang Kaehler

Cover photographs courtesy of Joe Yakura, (background) Michael Newman/Photo Edit

Special thanks to Dr. Yvonne Lau, education and research associate, office of the associate vice president for academic affairs at DePaul University; former director of Asian and Asian-American studies at Loyola University, Chicago; and founding president of the Asian American Institute in Chicago for her comments made in preparation of this book. The author wishes to thank the following people for all of their help: Dr. Joe Yakura, Dr. Ikuko Anjo Jassey, Nina Streitfeld, Mami Fujita, and Brian Krumm.

Some quotations and material used in this book come from the following source. In some cases, quotes have been abridged or edited for clarity: pp. 13, 17 *Coming to America: Immigrants from the Far East* by Linda Perrin (New York: Delacorte Press, 1980).

For more information on the people on the cover of this book, turn to page 4. A photo of a Little Tokyo neighborhood in Los Angeles, California, where many Japanese Americans live and work, is shown in the background.

Contents

Some words are shown in bold, **like this.** You can find out what they mean by looking in the glossary.

Susumu Comes to the United States

In June 1964 Susumu Yakura was preparing for a ten-day boat trip from Japan to the United States. He was twelve years old. A ship called the *Braziru-maru* would take him and his family to the U.S. to join his father. His parents decided to move so their children could go to college. College was very expensive in Japan. Susumu's father believed he could afford to send his children to college in the U.S.

The Yakura family had lived in Susumu's hometown near Yonago, Japan, for ten generations. They are shown here at the Yonago train station on their journey to the United States.

Susumu was happy in Japan. He would rush home from school each day and play baseball or go fishing with friends. Like many Japanese **immigrants,** he knew he would miss his friends when he moved. But he was still excited to move to the U.S. Relatives he had never met lived there. Also, his grandmother had lived in California for several years. She had told him about Disneyland and about famous actors who lived in Hollywood.

Shortly after the Yakuras moved to California, Susumu got to see Disneyland for himself.

The ship ran into huge waves for about two days during our voyage. I remember many adults got **seasick** at that time.
—Susumu Yakura

Japan

Japan is a country made up of many islands in the Pacific Ocean. It is near the east coast of Asia. The land in Japan has many mountains and more than 60 volcanoes. Much of that land cannot be lived on. Most people in Japan live in the plains and valleys in Japan. As a result, a lot of people live on a very small area of land. Having more land to live on is one reason Japanese people **immigrated** to the United States.

In Japanese, the country's name is *Nippon* or *Nihon,* which means "source of the sun."

These Japanese farmers grew rice in the late 1800s in Japan.

6

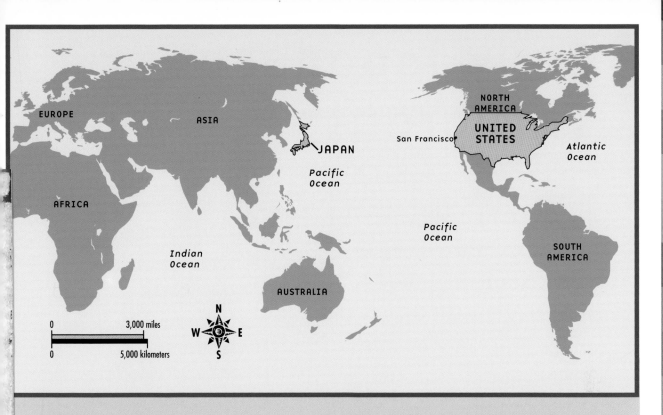

Many early Japanese immigrants sailed about 7,000 miles (11,265 kilometers) across the Pacific Ocean to San Francisco, California.

Many Japanese people were farmers in Japan. They had been farming the same lands for centuries. In the late 1800s, huge factories were built on what had been their farmlands. They feared that they would never be able to make money in this changing country. Some Japanese people started looking for different lands where they could farm.

Japan opened their **ports** and began doing business with the United States in 1854. Matthew Perry of the U.S. Navy forced Japan's government leaders to sign a trade agreement.

7

Early Japanese Immigrants

Japan started allowing people to move away in 1886. Many Japanese farmers thought they could make more money in the United States than they ever could in Japan. Most of the people who left Japan planned to return after saving money. However, few of those who **immigrated** actually went back.

Many of the first Japanese immigrants went to Hawaii to work on sugar cane **plantations.** When Hawaii became a U.S. **territory** in 1898, the children of these Japanese workers became the first Japanese Americans.

On July 25, 1920, these Japanese girls arrived in the United States aboard a ship called the Shinyu Maru.

These Japanese people came to the U.S. in 1920. They went from Japan to San Francisco.

The trip across the Pacific Ocean was long and difficult. Most Japanese immigrants could only afford to buy **steerage** class tickets. They spent the three-week journey in crowded rooms at the bottom of a ship. Those who went directly to the United States arrived at a **port** in San Francisco, California.

Time Line

1899	More than 65,000 Japanese workers live in Hawaii.
1900–1910	More than 140,000 Japanese immigrants arrive in the United States.
1924	The U.S. bans immigration from Japan.
1942–1945	More than 100,000 Japanese Americans are forced to live in **internment camps** during **World War Two**.
1952	Japanese immigrants are allowed to become U.S. citizens.

Arriving in the United States

Japanese **immigrants** who arrived in San Francisco were taken to an immigration station called Angel Island. There they were questioned about their plans. They were also checked by doctors to be sure they were healthy. Those who were sick often had to pay for treatment at a hospital. Other Japanese people who were sick were sent back to Japan.

These Japanese women had to answer questions and be checked by doctors before they could enter the United States.

This map shows some of the areas that Japanese immigrants first came to and where many Japanese Americans still live today.

From Angel Island, the immigrants traveled on boats to San Francisco. Many stayed in California where they found jobs. Others traveled to the Pacific Northwest, settling in Oregon and Washington.

Some Japanese-American men arranged to marry women who lived in Japan. These women came to the U.S. to meet their husbands. They were called "picture brides" because often the man and woman had only seen pictures of each other. One reason that some Japanese Americans married picture brides was because there were laws that said they could not marry white American women.

11

Life in the United States

By 1910, more than 150,000 Japanese people had **immigrated** to the United States. Most of them lived in California. There they found jobs working on farms and building railroads. Some Japanese immigrants worked as gardeners and **domestic servants.** The average pay for one of these jobs was not much—$1 to $1.50 a day. But in Japan in the 1890s, the average pay for workers was about fourteen cents a day.

A section of Los Angeles came to be known as Little Tokyo. There, Japanese immigrants and Japanese Americans owned **boarding houses,** grocery stores, and other shops.

This Japanese-American boy helped gather carrots on a farm in California.

This photo, taken in about 1919, shows Jackson Street in Seattle, Washington. Many Chinese and Japanese immigrants opened shops and businesses on this street.

Many Japanese immigrant farmers had to **lease** farmland because there were laws in some states that said they could not own land. Still, in California, Japanese immigrants were very successful farmers. They drained land that other people had thought would never be good for farming. They even started growing rice in California—something earlier farmers there had not been able to do. They also grew strawberries, peppers, and grapes.

Japanese farmers and laborers came to Little Tokyo for lots of reasons . . . especially to get things from Japan. In the old days you [could not] even get rice outside of Little Tokyo.
—a Japanese immigrant who lived in Little Tokyo

Problems in the United States

Despite problems and challenges that Japanese **immigrants** had to overcome, many found success in the United States. But some people in the U.S. were not happy about that success. Other Americans judged Japanese people. Some thought that Japanese immigrants did not have the same **values** as they did.

This sign in Livingston, California, said, "No More Japanese Wanted Here." It was put up in the early 1900s by a person who probably thought Japanese immigrants were taking jobs away from other Americans.

Some Americans tried to make the children of Japanese immigrants go to their own separate schools. These children are shown in a classroom in California in 1927.

In 1906, city leaders in San Francisco tried to create a separate school system for Japanese-American children. Japanese Americans were angered. They wanted their children to be like other Americans—to speak English, wear American clothes, and attend American schools. U.S. government leaders said that Japanese-American children did not have to attend separate schools. **Discrimination** continued in other ways, however.

Japanese immigrants were not allowed to become American citizens until 1952.

Wartime Camps

Discrimination against Japanese Americans rose dramatically in the 1940s. The world was fighting **World War Two,** and the United States and Japan were on opposite sides. Some Americans thought that Japanese Americans were spies. But no Japanese American was ever arrested for spying. Even so, on February 9, 1942, U.S. President Franklin D. Roosevelt signed an **order** that said all Japanese Americans had to move to **internment camps.**

Many young Japanese-American men volunteered for the U.S. military and fought in all-Japanese units.

About 117,000 Japanese Americans were forced to live in internment camps between 1942 and 1945. The camps were in areas of California, Arizona, Idaho, Utah, Wyoming, Colorado, and Arkansas. The camp in the photo is in Santa Anita, California.

Air forces from Japan bombed Pearl Harbor, a U.S. military base in Hawaii, in 1941. The day after the bombing, a Japanese-American shop owner put this sign on his shop front in Oakland, California.

Japanese Americans had to sell their homes and belongings before they moved to the camps. Six families usually lived in each building at the camps. There was little privacy in the buildings. Sound traveled easily between rooms. Not even the bathrooms offered a place to be alone. There were no walls between the showers or toilets. The U.S. government closed the camps after the war ended.

I would do anything for the United States, even risk my life. I had children who were United States citizens and I wanted them to be proud of me, so when I was in camp I volunteered to do something to win the war.

—Roy Yano, a Japanese **immigrant**

Immigration Continues

In 1952, the United States government reviewed the **immigration** rules they had made in 1924. A new law was passed that said people could once again come to the U.S. from Japan and become U.S. citizens. However, only 100 people were allowed into the U.S. each year. That limit ended in 1965 and large numbers of Japanese immigrants began arriving in the United States. Today, about 5,000 Japanese immigrants come to the United States each year.

Sometimes Japanese families move to the U.S. after the mother or father gets a new job there.

18

Many recent Japanese immigrants work as doctors and scientists, such as this Japanese-American woman.

The largest numbers of Japanese Americans still live in Hawaii and California, where the earliest immigrants lived. Since the 1960s, Japanese Americans have moved east. Illinois and New York both have large Japanese-American populations. Recent Japanese immigrants work at all types of jobs, including as businesspeople, scientists, and teachers.

When the **internment camps** closed, most Japanese Americans returned to their lives in the United States. Some felt they had been treated too unfairly and decided to return to Japan.

Japanese Arts and Traditions

Over the years, Japanese Americans have introduced the United States to many Japanese **traditions.** One tradition that Japanese **immigrants** brought to the United States is a form of gardening. It is called bonsai. Bonsai is the growing and trimming of **miniature** trees. It takes patience and practice to learn how to trim and shape the trees. Bonsai is also thought to help strengthen a person's love of nature.

In *The Karate Kid,* Japanese-American actor Noriyuki "Pat" Morita showed how to trim a bonsai tree.

This photo shows how small some of the trees used in bonsai gardening are.

This Japanese-American woman is teaching origami to her granddaughter.

Another traditional art form that Japanese immigrants brought to the United States is origami. Origami is art created by folding paper. Usually, one sheet of paper is used. The paper is not cut, only folded. Many origami designs are of items found in nature. The most common designs are for cranes, a type of bird with a long neck.

Origami is very delicate and takes a lot of patience.
—Kei Karasaki, a Japanese-American woman who grew up in Connecticut

Celebrations

New Year's is a big celebration for people all over the world. In Japan, schools and businesses are closed from January 1 to January 3 so that people can celebrate New Year's. New Year's is called *Oshogatsu* in Japan. Japanese Americans celebrate *Oshogatsu* in the United States as well. The *Oshogatsu* celebration includes many Japanese **customs.** One custom is to eat *mochi,* a type of rice cake. *Mochi* takes a very long time to prepare. First, rice is pounded into a paste. Then, the paste is shaped into flat cakes.

This Japanese-American boy in Hawaii made mochi *rice cakes on New Year's Day.*

*Japanese Americans have been enjoying **traditional** Japanese celebrations in the U.S. for a long time. This photo shows a Girls' Day festival that was held in about 1930 in California.*

Some Japanese-American children celebrate *Hinamatsuri,* or Girls' Day, and *Tango-no-sekku,* or Boys' Day. Young children do something special on these days. For Girls' Day, girls usually dress in **kimonos.** Then, they visit their friends and have a tea party with their dolls. On Boys' Day, families with sons fly large banners that are shaped like fish. Usually, one banner is flown for each boy in the family.

In the Kitchen

Japanese **immigrants** introduced new foods to the United States. Japanese people have developed many ways to serve fish and other seafood. One of those ways is known as **sushi.** Sushi is rice flavored with sweet vinegar—a liquid commonly served on salads in the U.S. Often, a piece of seaweed is used to wrap the rice around raw fish or vegetables. There are restaurants throughout the U.S. that only serve sushi.

The Japanese word *sushi* actually means "with rice," not "raw fish" as many people believe.

This Japanese-American cook served sushi to a woman at a restaurant in Los Angeles.

Diners at this hibachi restaurant in Little Rock, Arkansas, are entertained by the chef preparing their meals.

Hibachi restaurants have also become popular in the United States. At hibachi restaurants, meals are cooked right at the tables. There are hot metal grills in the centers of the tables. A chef prepares all of the food while standing at the table. The chef cuts seafood, vegetables, and meat and even tosses them in the air. These chefs often amaze the people watching them.

In 1964, Japanese American Hiroaki "Rocky" Aoki opened his first hibachi restaurant in New York. It was named after his parents' coffee shop in Japan—Benihana, which means "red flower." There are now more than 90 Benihana restaurants worldwide.

Two Cultures

Learning about American **culture** has been very important to Japanese **immigrants.** But they also have great pride in Japanese culture. Many Japanese immigrants gave their children American-sounding names, such as Eugene or Linda. At the same time, many Japanese-American parents send their children to special schools to learn how to speak Japanese and about Japanese culture.

When I was a kid, I was really unhappy about having to go to Japanese school on Saturdays while my American friends were enjoying their weekend. But being fluent in Japanese after spending more than half of my life in America more than makes up for all the sleepovers I missed.
—Mami Fujita, who came to the U.S. from Japan when she was 8

*These Japanese Americans played **traditional** Japanese drums at a cultural festival in Los Angeles.*

*These people are shown wearing **kimonos** in Seattle, Washington.*

The Japanese have names for each generation of immigrant families. The immigrants are called Issei. Their American-born children are called Nisei. Children of the Nisei are called Sansei.

Some Japanese-American children spend part of their childhoods in Japan. The children live with family members in Japan. Many people think that the best way to learn about a country and its culture is to live there for a period of time.

Joe Yakura Today

Susumu started using the name Joe when he arrived in California. At school, he had a hard time understanding his teachers at first. But as he learned more English, they started to make sense to him. Joe decided he wanted to be a lawyer. To be a lawyer, he would have to do a lot of speaking. Unfortunately, speaking English was difficult for Joe.

Since my dad was a **self-employed** gardener, we ended up helping him whenever we had off from school. I used to hate holidays because it was much easier to go to school than help with his work.   —Joe Yakura

Joe is seen here in the center with his brothers, Osamu (left) and Jack (right), in 1984.

28

Joe and his wife Mayumi visited Washington, D.C., in 1996.

He had always done well at math and science, though, even in Japan. So, Joe decided to become a physicist, which is a type of scientist. Like many Japanese Americans, Joe has found success in the United States. He was not only able to go to college. He also continued his education to the highest level. Joe works for the United States Air Force today. He lives in New Mexico and works as a physicist.

Joe returned to Japan on several occasions as part of his job. While he was there, he met his wife Mayumi.

Japanese Immigration Chart

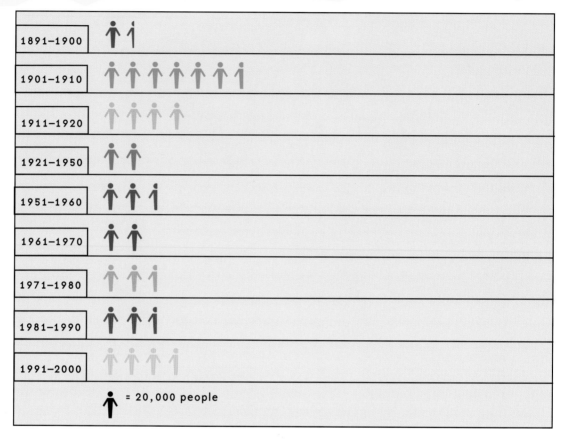

1891–1900	
1901–1910	
1911–1920	
1921–1950	
1951–1960	
1961–1970	
1971–1980	
1981–1990	
1991–2000	

= 20,000 people

*More than half a million people **immigrated** to the United States from Japan from 1891 to 2000.*

Source: U.S. Immigration and Naturalization Service

More Books to Read

Contino, Jennifer M. *The Japanese Americans.* Broomall, Pa.: Mason Crest, 2003.

Emery, Vivian. *I Am Japanese American.* New York: Rosen Publishing, 1997.

MacMillan, Dianne M. *Japanese Children's Day and the Obon Festival.* Berkeley Heights, N.J.: Enslow Publishers, 1997.

Perl, Lila. *Behind Barbed Wire.* New York: Benchmark Books, 2002.

Glossary

boarding house building in which bedrooms are rented and meals are served

culture ideas, skills, arts, and way of life for a certain group of people

custom way that people have done certain things for a long time

discrimination unfair treatment of people because of where they are from, how they look, or what they believe

domestic servant person who works in another's home, usually as a maid

immigrate to come to a country to live there for a long time. A person who immigrates is an immigrant.

internment camp area that Japanese Americans had to move to after Japanese forces attacked a U.S. military base, Pearl Harbor, on December 7, 1941

kimono loose robe with wide sleeves worn as an outer garment by the Japanese

lease make regular payments to use something that you do not own

miniature copy of something at much smaller size

order statement or command made by the government or other officials

plantation large farm where crops are grown by workers who live there

port city near water where ships dock and leave from

seasick sick in the stomach due to a ship's rocking motion

self-employed working for oneself, or having one's own business or company

steerage place on a ship where passengers who pay the least to travel stay

sushi type of food that includes rice, vegetables, and sometimes raw fish wrapped in seaweed

territory large division or area of a nation. People who live in a territory have some but not all of the same rights that citizens of the nation do.

tradition belief or practice handed down through the years from one generation to the next

value what people think is special or important in life

World War Two war fought from 1939 to 1945 by Germany, Japan, and Italy on one side and the United States, Great Britain, China, Poland, France, and the Soviet Union on the other

Index